# Lens

Rachel Walters

Presentation by *BookLeaf Publishing*

Web: www.bookleafpub.com

E-mail: info@bookleafpub.com

ISBN: 9789357211901

First edition 2023

# DEDICATION

I dedicate this to my children...


Your tiny hands have held on so tight to kept me afloat over the last several years. Please know I am sincerely sorry for the decisions I've made, and I will continue making better ones to become who you need me to be. I love you both so very much.

# ACKNOWLEDGEMENT

I would like to acknowledge all the people out there struggling in silence. I know it isn't always easy to ask for help, but please try. There are kindhearted people hidden in this world who are able to love you in the ways you need to be loved and willing to walk beside you as you find your way back home.

I would not be here today had I not asked for help.

# PREFACE

The last several years of my life have been the most difficult years of my life. Loss, grieving over the living and the deceased, addictions, a break up, multiple heartaches, abuse, escaping death and becoming sober... This year has been truly one of a kind.

# Like You

I tend to see in others the way I view myself
I see the pain and laughter in stories they refuse to tell

But I would never pressure anyone to share them with me
I know talking about your problems never truly sets you free

In this narcissistic world where everyone is all about themselves,
My story is just another book collecting dust on a long forgotten shelf

However, I still have compassion to give to those who are around
Because I know how it feels to be alive while your soul is gasping underground

It's not an easy thing to do, but I know that you will always find a way
To continuously spread the love and light you contain inside everyday

The world needs more people like you

# Home

You were born an animal
Slowly tamed over time
Molded by your pain
Shamed by your joy
Maimed viciously by life
Your soul is placed 6ft under
While you're still alive forced
To live the life of a walking corpse

You find yourself in pieces
Searching for who you were
Supposed to be among the
Shattered mess on the floor
You so desperately wish
To be pieced back together
But instead you cry in silence
Afraid you'll cut your hands

Now you're screaming for help
But there is no one near
You can't live this way any longer
Time to make a critical decision
Neither of them will be easy
And you must do it on your own
It will ultimately make you
Or eventually break you again

Do you stay dead inside?
To exist meaninglessly
Lost without any direction
Be wandering aimlessly
With no protection, stagnant

No drive or no passion
A life without purpose
Is a life without action

Or do you fill that dark void?
Hunting for things that
Provide a sense of reason
To repaint your world
Expressively without fear
To love and be loved while
Slowly coming back to life
Finding your way back home

# The One

I was the one standing behind the camera, not in front
Capturing candid moments I thought you'd wish to reminisce
I was the one waiting for you to return home to eat dinner
So you didn't have to sit at the table by yourself
I was the one designing and making handmade gifts because
There was nothing in a store that seemed to get you
I was the one leaving little love notes hidden around the house
To surprise you as you found them reminding you of my love
I was the one who kept suggesting things for us to do together
To avoid watching the same show on Netflix for the 50th time
I was the one who would roll over towards you once we laid down
Just to be as close as physically possible to fuse into one being
I was the one who kept arguing even when you would walk away
Because I would have given my last breath fighting for you
I was the one who never let you sleep on the couch after a quarrel
Because nothing was worth missing a night by your side

I was the one who
Stopped taking pictures
Stopped waiting to eat
Stopped creating gifts
Stopped leaving notes

I was the one who
Started over season one
Started to face away
Started to choose silence
Started to sleep on the couch

# Her

At the time, everything around us was literally coming
undone
The house, our love, our minds, and likely my liver
I think our last drug of choice put the final nail in the coffin
But I never thought you would ever run to her
Despite all the complaints, you continue to create a new life
Ten yards away from our home in the neighbors house
Which could only lead me to wonder and question
If and for long you guys were sneaking around
You used to tell me stories of you two growing up together
And you never really had anything good to say
Yet now you sleep in her bed holding her every night
And tell me you still love me during the day
Then say you would like to spend some time with us
Which was a slight shock, but no big deal to me
I was glad that you came and our kids got to see you
Until I saw your neck stained with hickeys

You say you started dating a few months after we split
But you'll have to excuse me for thinking that is a lie
Because I always thought you had some secrets
Now I feel like this very well could have been why
The kicker is when you told me how you guys linked
And the reason why you even went over to her house
You explained to me that her ol' man was beating on her
So you assertively stepped in and ran the guy out
Don't get me wrong, I'm glad that you did even though
I've never liked her since day one before all of this
But absolutely no one deserves to be bruised by love
And there is nothing in this world that could ever justify it
However, there is one thing that I can't quite grasp
Please forgive me if this is out of line, but I don't see

How you could save her from a man like that
When you were that same man to me?

# Seedlings

Things were great in the beginning just like new loves always are
All the difficulties started to surface which inevitably tore us apart
I should have left long ago, like the day you said you didn't love me
But I knew it came from a place of hurt 'cuz you would never say something so ugly
Then the toughest battle came that pushed my back into the wall
I lost both my heart and soul that day because I tried to keep you all
Yet we did what we could to find ways to bring us all together
To find shelter within each other through the messiest of weather
A couple years went by and it seemed like the compliance to everything we did
Wasn't good enough to unify under one roof, I think that's when the devil placed his bid
I should have left again then but I didn't want to lose you too
The gavel banged at that mistake, I know, because the living hell that put us through
Yet resiliently through trial and error, we continued searching for the reason
Why we fell in love in the first place but only ended with me charged of treason
I knew it was solely my fault, and mine alone, though I tried to place blame on you
That's why kept myself drunk enough to numb the guilt I ate from serving that pain to you

Though you tried to forgive me, we both knew it wouldn't be the same
But for some reason we couldn't stop roleplaying as two fools in cupids game
And the more we tried to become close, it only made the distance grow
Even on the nights of fiery passion, it still felt ice cold
By this point there was no denying that our relationship was doomed
That staying together may as well been equal to rubbing salt into fresh wounds
We got tangled in a venomous web hoping we would bond by energy
But honestly all it actually did was violently propel us to our ending
We lost sight of what really mattered bringing about hateful words and physical abuse
Though I secretly felt like I deserved it all for those nights I ripped your heart in two
I never thought we would break up, we stuck so long through the thick of it
There had to have been something truly there for us to not forsaken it
After six years shared, I see it may have been the right person but the wrong time
Or possibly the other way around, nonetheless, I do regret some decisions of mine
I miss what we had before it hit the fan and wrapped around making things worse
However, I am thankful for how it ended simply because it could've been in a hearse
Even throughout our darkest nights, you were still my only best friend who
Was there for us and I know in both of our hearts that you are a good man

We were just young, dumb and in love, just seedlings that
needed the rain to grow
I'm finally able to let go of the past as I reach forward to
regaining my heart and soul

# Break It

If erasing your pain means breaking my heart,
Then by all means, break it
Break it any way you can
Find a million and one different ways to just
Break it
Tear it
Crumble it
Smash it
Fracture it
Shatter it
Demolish it
Obliterate it
Blow it to fucking smithereens
Over and over and over
If you have you
I don't care
Just promise me,
That you will not stop
Until there's absolutely
Nothing left until

You're happy again

# Dig

How do you long for love
Yet judge it at the same time?
You yearn for acceptance
And reject it within the same line

I loved you in my own ways
How dare you say it was never true?
I know that I'm not a fraud
Maybe it was just too real for you

I surrendered everything I had
To you like a thief in the night
You've taken everything from me
As you smothered my light

Were you ever truly deserving
Of all that I had to give?
I know how deep my love runs
You were just unwilling to dig

Not that you had to go far
Just maybe a foot or two
It's my own fault I'm hurt
For expecting anything from you

# Falling

Falling out of love... It's a long way from the top
Yet you never know you're falling until you land on your
face
The sudden realization that everything you knew is no
longer
Going from one extreme to the other without warning
From each deep breath fueling the fires that once burned
inside you
To gasping for air as your lungs fill with water
The busyness the butterflies thrived on eventually start to
calm
Causing their overworked wings to crumble in fragility
The blinding vibrancy of your unconditional love becomes
Dulled over time with by being used improperly over and
over
Precious and joyous things you once cared for above all the
rest
Sadly become dusty remnants of the past upon the highest
shelf
Witnessing a home supported by strong, beautifully
decorated walls
Being carelessly torn apart piece by piece until it's fully
demolished
Gentle thoughts that once brought purpose and motivation
unknowingly
Change their tone leaving behind with you a defeated heart
From happily spending hours doing things that suffused
you with passion
To become unable to enjoy a single second of it... Or of
anything at all
While mercifully wishing the reaper would come to your
door

I always hear people say, falling in love is easy and
painless,
And it will find us only when it is meant to be
Well, I'm beginning to believe that is a crock of shit
While you've been descending for what feels like forever
You forget who are you are in all the chaos and destruction
on your way down
Alone and at rock bottom is where you will meet your true
self
You have to have the want, the will and find the way to
attain love again
And it will be the most difficult journey you will ever
endure
Breaking the routine of your toxic cycles and habits,
Feeling the discomfort of new and forgotten territories
Embracing those horrible memories and emotions that
made you with for death
Hating those dreadful seconds until you sincerely love
them,
Smoothing those calluses even if causes new ones to form,
Rebuilding those walls stronger and more glorious than
before,
Overcoming your fear of heights as you climb the ladder to
reach the top shelf,
Remembering how to give unrequited love especially to
those who don't deserve it,
The patience needed to rehabilitate those wings as a new
generation of butterflies emerge,
Choking until you cough out the water so you can finally
breathe again,
It will not be easy, but I can guarantee it will be worth it

I hope you fall back in love with living

# The Call

It never stops ringing
Even on silent, I can still hearing the dinging

There it is again
Demons from my past disguised as a friend

I let it go to voicemail
Avoiding any chance of reliving that hell

It rings again immediately
I blacken screen hoping it will leave me be

I can tell it's getting mad
But I don't care, I want to forget what we had

It's annoyingly persistent
I hit the "fuck you" button without any resistence

Again? This is crazy
Just give up already and cut your ties with me

After several more attempts
I lose every bit my composure and finally submit

What is it you could possibly want?!
The sound of nothingness begins to tease and taunt

After the long pause,
A menacing chuckle brings the silence to a halt

The sound involuntarily
Sends chills down my spine, almost seductively

Click.

# The Hang Up

I haven't been able to stop thinking about it
That foreboding laugh has played on loop
It has been well over two days now
But I have not figured out how to recoup

And even though it hasn't called since
I can still hear the tone playing in my head
It's really beginning to take a toll on me
So I decided to call it back this time instead

Spitefully, it does to me what I did to it
Refusing to acknowledge me until I see red
So I keep on calling and calling and calling
Until my battery is dead

# Eye Contact

It's almost as if there is someone peeking through your
window
Watching you dance in all your naked glory, completely
exposed
You know there isn't anyone there, but you can't shake the
eeriness
The trepidation convincingly creeps its way into a full
embrace
What if there is someone there? What exactly could they
see?
Naturally, you must check to appease your curiosity and
worries
As you tiptoe towards the window, you begin to second
guess
Mustering the courage, you slowly separate the slats, ever
so gently
Only to be greeted by two eyes staring back at you

Your own eyes widen as your face turns pale, thrusting
back in fright
Damn near ripping the curtains off the rod trying to pull
them shut
Adrenaline fills your veins as you stumble over your own
two feet
Recklessly throwing things to the floor in hopes of creating
an obstacle
Turning off every light on the way, as you frantically run to
the
Furthest corner in the room where you minimize yourself to
hide
Your heart contends vigorously to keep up with your rapid
breathing

The violent trembling beneath your silky skin makes you
feel as if
Your joints will somehow loosen enough for your skeleton
to fall apart

But all they could see was,

You standing there with your toes quirkily pointed inward
and
How it causes you to stand with your weight shifted to one
side
Prompting one knee to slightly bend so elegantly in front of
the other
How your waist slowly rocks back and forth like a boat on
a calm lake
How your hands sensuously move around, hugging
different parts
Of your body as if they have no idea what to do with
themselves
Enjoying the random placement of the warm freckles that
lay gracefully
Upon porcelain skin with softly painted rose colored cheeks
that
Bubble from the tender smile of love stretching across your
face

All the while refusing to let them dive into your pools of
honey as
You tell them your favorite color

# Stained

A single sheet, crystal clear
Once transparent and dull
Lacking any imperfections
Is broken into segments
That are delicately handled
Cuts are made with precision
For a much greater purpose
Each piece is painted with intent
Enduring the fire proves its worthiness
To proudly display the bold colors
Placed within and held together by
The iron veins that embrace each
Elaborately complex shard
Reducing its fragility
Ultimately producing
A single magnificent design

# Drown

I've tried for so long to keep my head above water
Trying to escape the undertows of mind and heart
Where, no matter what, I'm caught by one or the other
Flailing around, trying to escape
Ultimately making it worse
One side is rational, analyzing everything
Controlling my breathing, keeping predators away,
Making sure I don't accidently intake any water
While the other is desperately convincing, urging me
To curve the hunger pangs if only for a moment
Either way, I could dehydrate so why not pacify one
Despite the consequences?

To know right from wrong is common sense, yet a burden
Wading and waiting in the vastness with no direction
I catch a glimpse of a tiny boat in the distance and
I keep trying to swim my way over but it seems
The current is much stronger than I can handle
I couldn't imagine any waves for I'm exhausted as it is
Storm clouds begin to roll in as the sky grow dark
I've done nothing by try with all I had this entire time
And yet I feel further from shore now than ever
My body gives and I stop moving my arms and legs
Everything around me seems more relaxed and natural
Drifting away freely without my all franticness and
I finally understand how calming the waters can be

If I would have just let myself drown

# Nocturnal Rainbow

I was always afraid of the dark and what was in it
Rejection, failure, uncertainty within the void
Never fully knowing where I stood when
I couldn't even see my hand in front of my face

That's when I realized I couldn't stay there
I had to turn on a light to be able to see myself
But the thought alone terrified me because then,
You'd be able to see me too

I desire to be accepted and loved for who I am
Be free in my expression and success except
I'm too much of a coward to fully expose myself
Simply in fear of being thrown back into the abyss

It's a vicious cycle that's starting to impair my sight
Like someone endlessly flipping on and off a switch
All the adjusting brings physical pain to the point
I just clench my eyes shut and hide behind a shade of red

Is my fear of falling truly greater than the possibility of
flying?
Do I even deserve to feel that type of unconditional love
With all the hurt I've caused? Does the joy people say
I've brought into their lives even matter?

Does it amount to anything?
Is it not good enough yet?
Would it eventually balance out?
Could it ever?

It's much easier to ignore ugliness in the dark

When you can't confront the things you don't wish to see
While missing all the beauty at the same time

Rainbows are undeniably visible during the day
But who's to say they aren't there at night?

# Window Pain

What exactly is a window?
Individual panes of glass
Held together within a frame
Transforming it as a whole
Requiring constant maintenance
In efforts to prevent any and all
Blemishes deemed as a
Deterrence to your hopeful gaze
A manipulation of focus
Making you blind to the outside

What can I see from my windows?
Steam from tears that produced a fog
With such impenetrable density
Making me feel lost and knee deep in mud
Coats of dust forming from stagnancy
Disastrous gusts of humbling cruelty
Creating a sparkling pile of debris with
Intent of restoring my ability to absorb
The beauty that is beyond the pane
In spite of the jagged remainders

# You'll Never Know

The world will never love you the way that I do
Their hearts won't skip an extra beat like mine when I catch
you smiling at yourself
They'll never know the warmth of your flesh on the coldest
of nights
Or exactly how high or low your chest rises and falls with
every breath

They'll never hear what you actually meant to say in your
jumbled mess of words
Their eyes won't recognize the silent pain in yours that
you've buried so deeply
Their hands aren't nearly big enough to bother holding all
your troubles
Or as soft and nurturing as mine to soothe your worries
away

They'll never feel the undertones of your voice in their
bones during the morning hours
They'll never be moved by the depth of your passion for the
things that fulfill your soul
They'll never see the light struggling to shine inside while
you sit alone in the dark
Or be able to fathom how incredibly worth it and deserving
you are

You'll never know a love like mine, and unfortunately you
won't know it now…
How can I give all this to someone else when I don't feel it
towards myself?
It isn't fair to make it someone else's burden to carry

Maybe by the end of eternity, I'll be worthy enough for a
love like mine

However, that's quite some time from now and I'd never
ask you to wait
But if by chance you decided to stay around, I promise
once that day comes
I will love both of us infinitely

# Frame

Why did I sniffle away the agony?
Did it bury the feelings of death inside me,
Or did it bring me fleeting moments of feeling alive?

Why did I drown my guilt and sorrows?
Did I drink enough to sink the ship that carried my pain,
Or did it cause the wreckage to come crashing to the shore?

Why did I purposely bring myself pain?
Did the breach of my flesh prevent a disastrous flood,
Or did it allow me to relieve the overflow little by little?

Why did I tell myself I wasn't good enough?
Did those words provide a twisted sense of stability,
Or did extreme modesty make me feel unworthy?

Why did I stay in a place where I didn't belong?
Did stagnancy coagulate into a solid foundation to stand,
Or did it clip my wings before I could even learn to fly?

Why did I not walk away from people?
Did it create the boundaries and limitations I hold for
myself,
Or did it show that my love can be truly unconditional?

Everything happens for a reason and
Everyone chooses their own lens and
Everything is perfect exactly as is

All these things happen for us to
Learn how to strengthen the frame
That will hold the masterpiece within

# Bubble

It's comfortable in here
I like my bubble

Dark
Unable to absorb the unpretty around me
Solitude
Ecstasy of having my own private space
Peaceful
Shunning out the unnecessary chaos
Quiet
Allows me to hear my own thoughts
Reunite
Where I finally get to meet her again

Inquisition leads to exploration
Concluding with the realization

She isn't how I remember

This mirrored sphere contorts my view
As I scream back defensively at the voices
There is nothing to distract me from her
The bubble shrinks as the void grows
Saturated rays of ugliness breach from
Inside so violently ensuring I stay blind

I don't like it anymore
It's terrifying in here

# Midnight Angels

They are the ones who sit beside you
Beneath the softness of a pale moon
With a gentle luminous glow amidst the void
Gifting you peace after the chaos of the day
Untangling the knots in your stomach
Sorting the clutter compiled in your mind
Lightening the burdens in your heart
Giving you the freedom you to release
Your regrets from yesterday
Your anguish of today and
Your worries of tomorrow
In hopes you sleep peacefully tonight
Leaving you with promises of their return
No matter how long it seems to take
Or how great the distance becomes
They will arrive again in your darkest hours
To ensure your tears never fall in solitude
After all the laughter you've shared together
Doing their best to collect every drop so
They may provide nourishment to the roots
Of the beauty that will bloom again at dawn

# Calm

You're like…

Eating fresh pineapple while watching the sunset paint the
clouds on a midsummer evening
The tranquilizing ebb and flow of cool blue waves softly
washing over the tops of my feet
Being in the eye of a hurricane while the ferocity of a
destructive storm circles around me
The relief found within the walls of a cozy cabin from the
glacier winds that sting your face
An escape from the world as you enter a new galaxy built
by the pages within your hands
That one specific song that comforts your weary soul as if
it was composed just for you
The chill beneath the shady oak tree that provides fleeting
shelter from the blistering sun
Choosing to take the scenic way home after a dreadful day
in spite of the extra time it costs
The loveliness of lilacs filling your lungs until the
redolence ascends you to the heavens
Awakening in a tenebrous room during the winter but being
blissfully warm under the covers
Cathartically singing in the shower while witnessing your
worries spiral down the drain
Relaxing on the front porch listening to dahlias gulp the
rain to quench their thirsty roots
A protective embrace when the sky seems to be
plummeting down like an endless meteor shower
Rhythmically swaying with the breeze between the pines as
you drift away into wonderland

Yeah…

You're like all that
And a bag of chips

# Dahlia

On your journey to open the golden oak doors
You noticed something outlandish in the borders
Beneath the clusters of marigolds and begonias

Just as you were leaning down for a closer look
An overcast of rolling thunder and crying clouds
Steadily seized the warm light from the sun

You ran inside shutting the doors behind you
And ran just as quickly to the nearest window
To witness the storm through fogged panes

After some time passed and the sky was relit
You ventured back out to observe the damage
Taking notice again to the edges of the path

The marigolds were mangled, wilted and helpless
The begonias were broken, jaded and lifeless
Some destroyed, some derooted, all left there to die

Except the lone pariah that stole your attention
Bashfully hiding below the dense, colorful canopy
Standing modestly despite the gales and rain bombs

Even still with injured petals and a warped stem,
You were in awe of the beauty and strength it held
And believed the midnight dahlia was worth saving